a

HOT AIR
BALLOON

is big.

a
CLOUD
is big.

AUSTRALIA

is big.

the
MOON
is big.

the EARTH is big.

the
SUN
is big.

the
STAR
POLLUX
is big.

the
MILKY WAY
GALAXY,

which is made of BILLIONS of stars
and BILLIONS of planets
and BILLIONS of other things
is REALLY, REALLY,
REALLY **BIG**—

but not
as **BIG** as the
M100
GALAXY

or a
GALAXY
CLUSTER!

so, are
YOU
big?
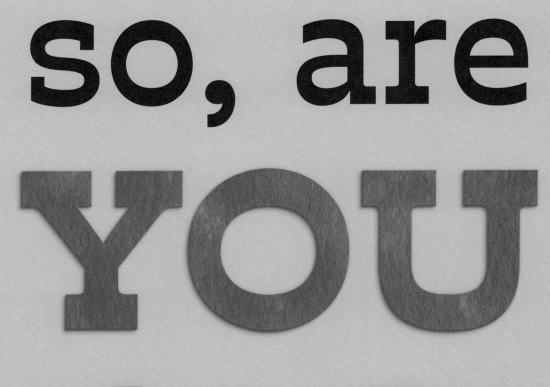

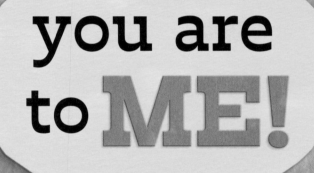

NEW YORK

UNION SQUARE KIDS and the distinctive Union Square Kids logo
are trademarks of Union Square & Co., LLC.

Union Square & Co., LLC, is a subsidiary of
Sterling Publishing Co., Inc.

Specific House

Text and illustrations © 2024 Mo Willems.
A Specific House book.

For information about custom editions, special sales,
and premium purchases, please contact
specialsales@unionsquareandco.com.

Printed in China
10 9 8 7 6 5 4 3 2 1

unionsquareandco.com

Design and image construction by Scott Sosebee.

This book is set in Trilby, UNSQ Sans, and Helvetica Neue LT Pro.

ISBN: 978-1-4549-4818-6

Library of Congress Control Number: 2022055953

**To Tim McKeon,
Kind of a Big Deal.**